VOICES FROM THE
HO CHI MINH TRAIL

VOICES FROM THE HO CHI MINH TRAIL

Poetry of America and Vietnam, 1965-1993

LARRY ROTTMANN

With Photographs by Nguyen Trong Thanh and Larry Rottmann

Foreword by Bruce Weigl

EVENT HORIZON PRESS • 1993

We wish to acknowledge the authors, editors and publishers of the following publications in which some of these poems have appeared: *Winning Hearts and Minds; The Lessons of the Vietnam War; A War Remembered; Front Lines; The New Soldiers; Vietnam in American Literature; Welcome to Cambridge; Carrying the Darkness; A New Anthology of Verse; Poems One Line and Longer; Approaches to Poetics; The Vietnam Wars; American Literature and the Experience of Vietnam; Vietnam: Anthology and Guide to a Television History; Illumination Rounds; Vietnam Generation; New Letters; Saturday Review; New Times; Soundings; Cornfield Review; Saigon Times; Bao Cuu Chien Binh; Saigon Giai Phong; Lao Dong; Van Nghe Quan Doi; Anthologie De La Litterature Vietnamienne.*

Note to Readers: The author's earnings from the sale of this book—along with those of photographer Nguyen Trong Thanh—are pledged to support the work of the non-profit Southeast Asia-Ozark Project, including the Jennings-Rottmann Memorial Scholarship Fund at Hue Medical University in Hue City, Vietnam. SEAOP's mission is to promote academic, cultural, and humanitarian dialogue and exchange between the people of the American midwest and the people of Indochina. SEAOP's address is: c/o Southwest Missouri State University, 901 South National Avenue, Springfield, Missouri 65804.

VOICES FROM THE HO CHI MINH TRAIL

Library of Congress Catalog Card Number 93-71258. ISBN 1-880391-06-6.

First Printing, September 1993.

Typography and design by Joseph Cowles. Bamboo illustrations adapted from a brush painting by Carol Warren.

Published by Event Horizon Press, Post Office Box 867, Desert Hot Springs, California 92240

∞ Printed and Bound in the United States of America.

SPECIAL THANKS

To these generous people and organizations for their crucial support in helping make this book possible:

My wife Francie and son Leroy; my parents Roy and Betty Cook Rottmann; Mark Biggs; Ray Castrey; Buzz Darby; E. Susanne Carter; Noam Chomsky; Chung Hoang Chuong; Zia Dina; Jeff Drake; W.D. Ehrhart; Marshall Gordon; Larry Heinemann; Harry Haines; Russell M. Keeling; Sister Agnes Lan; Prasit "Sid" Lohaviriyasiri; Ron Lunsford; Bernard Martell; Janice McCauley; Gene Michaud; Long T., Thien-Nga, and Thanh Nguyen; Huynh Quang Nhuong; Mike O'Brien; Jim Robertson; Bruce Weigl; The O.F. Kenworthy Southeast Asia-Ozark Project; Southwest Missouri State University; The Indochina Arts Project; The U.S.-Indochina Reconciliation Project; The William Joiner Center for the Study of War and Social Consequence; Vietnam Veterans Against the War (VVAW); 1st Casualty Press (1CP), Liberation News Service (LNS); the Vietnamese Mission to the United Nations; the United States Army; the Military Assistance Command (MACV).

And especially to Bob Linder, L.G. Patterson, David Pulliam, John Wall and Kevin White for their darkroom wizardry.

In Vietnam: Huynh Ngoc An; Mme. Nguyen Thi Binh; Hoang Kim Dang; Prof. Le Minh Dieu; Pham Van Hang; Vuong Khanh Hong; Col. Le Kim; Dr. Nguyen Hua Khoi; Le Thi Kim; Prof. Nguyen Lien; Van Luong; Le Luu; Nguyen Hong Nghi; Prof. Huu Ngoc; Van Sac; Nguyen Quang Sang; Hong Sen; Prof. Ngo Thi Phuong Thien; Nguyen Co Thach; Dr. Pham Nhu The; Tran Huu Thung; Dang Hoang Trung; Vietnam Tourism; the Union of Organizations for Peace, Solidarity and Friendship; the Center for Asia-Pacific Studies; the Vietnam Writers Union; the Ministry of Foreign Affairs; the Vietnam News Agency (VNA); the Peoples Army of Vietnam (PAVN); the Foreign Languages Publishing House—Hanoi.

And for their invaluable assistance with translations and insight: Dao Kim Hoa, Ly Thi Lan, Nguyen Quang Thieu, and many, many others.

Finally, with deepest appreciation to friend, colleague, and former brother-in-arms, Nguyen Trong Thanh, historian and photo artist for Vietnam Pictorial in Hanoi, who generously provided many of the photographs for this book.

For
Alice Herz
and
Thich Quang Duc

FOREWORD

Images of Vietnam have made their way gradually and in concussive and convoluted ways into the American consciousness. From the time of the earliest televised battlefield reports delivered to the citizens at supper, to the confused and angry voices of those soldiers who returned while the war still raged, and finally to our artistic and belles-lettristic responses, we have as a people begun to try to come to terms with what Vietnam meant to America during the war and what it continues to mean today.

As we approach the twentieth anniversary of the Paris Peace Accords, the bibliography of Vietnam War related literature in English has continually expanded to include literally thousands of works of fiction, nonfiction, poetry, drama, history, photo-essays, comic books and works of indeterminable genres. There have also been more than a dozen significant Hollywood motion pictures, and at least three major network television series, dealing directly with the war. In universities, colleges and high schools across the country, courses on "The Vietnam War" or "Vietnam War Literature" are being taught to a generation of students who were not yet born when their parents fought in the war, or against it. In fact, we have been so bombarded with images of Vietnam that we are perhaps in danger of being desensitized to the horrors of that war and its lingering legacy both here and in Vietnam.

Yet, somehow, we have not yet managed to get it right. Although some great literature has emerged in response to the war and has been rewarded with major literary prizes, even among those fine works, something has been missing, some significant parts of the story left out. The best of our Vietnam War literature, especially the fiction, embraces the horror of Vietnam and attempts at least to take fuller responsibility for that horror. This literature would include Tim O'Brien's *The Things They Carried* and *Going After Cacciato,* Larry Heinemann's *Paco's Story* and perhaps a dozen other works of fiction; and in nonfiction, Gloria Emerson's *Winners and Losers,* the first important book to bring the war home, gave voice to not only the troubled post-war veterans, but also to the mothers, fathers, wives and lovers of those lost in the war; and additionally, a few poetry anthologies, most notably *Winning Hearts and Minds,* edited by Larry Rottmann, Jan Barry and Basil Paquet, and *Unaccustomed Mercy,* edited by W. D. Ehrhart, provided forums for dozens of soldier-poets from the Vietnam War to tell their stories in such a variety of ways that their poems stitch together a kind of poetic history of American involvement in the war.

Conversely, the worst of what has been written in response to the war neither needs nor deserves little mention here. Suffice it to note that there have been far too many works of art produced in response to the war that have glorified in the suffering of others and romanticized the nightmare that war is. Among this cacophony of artistic responses, what's missing, ironically, is the presence of the Vietnamese themselves. Just as soldiers in training for the war were taught to dehumanize the Vietnamese so as to make it easier to kill them, the American public has not yet been allowed or able to imagine our former enemies in any other light but that of the faceless, nameless aggressor. Even in those works of art which have been widely accepted as accurate portrayals of the war, the Vietnamese have been so villainized that the most demeaning stereotype of yellow-skinned savages who have no regard for human life still pervades the minds of many Americans.

Even today, as we appropriately move toward reconciliation with Vietnam, there are those who continue to cling tenaciously to this racist view of the Vietnamese; insisting, for example, that they still hold American prisoners of war, and that our former enemies would, given the opportunity, slit our throats as we slept in our own beds. Many cultivate this image of the Vietnamese because they need to protect themselves from the unsettling truths of our involvement in that war: over fifty-eight thousand Americans dead, more than three-hundred thousand wounded, and over sixty thousand Vietnam vet suicides. And on the other side, as many as five million Vietnamese dead, two-thirds of whom were women and children. Allowing ourselves to see the Vietnamese as human beings would require us to accept more fully the responsibility for our individual and national actions during America's long involvement in Indochina.

This is exactly what Larry Rottmann forces us to do with this powerful and compelling account of his lengthy odyssey from college student to infantry officer to university teacher and Director of The O.F. Kenworthy Southeast Asia-Ozark Project, and finally as chronicler of the war and its aftermath.

Voices From The Ho Chi Minh Trail is

comprised of over ninety poems spanning nearly three decades, and more than a hundred photographs taken by Rottmann and his North Vietnamese counterpart, Nguyen Trong Thanh between 1965 and 1993. This book is a remarkable record of one veteran's life-long struggle to come to terms with just what Vietnam means to us as Americans, and even more important, to us as human beings. Just as Paul Fussell's *Great War and Modern Memory* argues that World War I forced the citizens of Great Britain to redefine what it means to be a civilized, humane people, Rottmann's book requires us to redefine what it means to be American, and thus represents a pinnacle of the recapitalization of heroic ideals.

Those who fought and survived the war can identify a change in themselves and in others who fought: a deadly surprised look in the eyes, a heavy and dark resolve that must have come with the recognition that the old way of thinking no longer worked; that there was no longer a hope commensurate to the forces which challenged hope; that their idealized notion of heroism had crumbled in the face of the brutality people were now clearly capable of inflicting upon one another.

Vietnam forced Larry Rottmann to recognize the otherness of other cultures, and brought him face-to-face with a people who were willing to fight bravely and die for ideals completely foreign to us. Those who fought and returned home from the war came back to discover a complete collapse of their moral identity; what they thought had been heroic battle, they came to realize, had actually been a dark absurdity perpetuated by the rich and powerful in ignorance and at the sake of a vast prodigality. Although the literature of the war has often been sub-categorized in such ways as to diminish its real power, a work like Rottmann's is arguably the most American of our recent literature for the way its capacity for moral understanding expands to include the chaos of Vietnam. It is a book that embraces the wholeness of what it means to be an American, and it does so not at the expense of the Vietnamese, but in a manner which humanizes them before our eyes in words and photographs.

Rottmann's book, however, is most significantly different from every other book in English about the war in its inclusion of the enemies' perspective. Seen most clearly in the so-called "voices" poems, Rottmann, during his many post-war trips to Vietnam, has managed to record the stories of North Vietnamese Regular and Viet Cong soldiers with amazing restraint and uncanny accuracy, so that we feel we are hearing the enemy speak for the first time about what the Vietnamese call the "American War." What emerges is not necessarily a patriotically-heroic portrait (although heroes are certainly present here), but a deeply human portrait. And what we can learn and come to understand about the Vietnamese who fought so valiantly against the American war machine is that they were very much like our own young soldiers: afraid, lonesome for home and loved ones, and engaged in an enterprise that they sometimes did not fully understand. This is the book's primary accomplishment and it should not be overlooked.

In its weakest form, the literary response to the Vietnam War will survive as sensationalist reportage, and will be eaten up by the commercial instincts of our literary business. At its best, however, in books like Rottmann's, this literature can teach us that to die alone and far from home for all the wrong reasons is not ever sweet or proper, and that there is nothing intrinsically patriotic about pulling the trigger, nothing glorious about combat.

And perhaps even more important, Rottmann's book can teach us by example that through art we can go on. Through the larger and more inclusive forms of the imagination we can somehow remain whole and can reconcile with ourselves, as well as with our former enemies.

Voices From The Ho Chi Minh Trail embodies, in fact, all of what art can do for us and teach us about ourselves: it sustains and passes on essential values; it teaches that violence is necessarily a part of our world, that there is no Eden without the serpent, that war has nothing to do with bravery; it celebrates the language by which we speak, imagine, love, hate, bless and curse daily; and it proves that even in the midst of overwhelming odds, a radiance, a triumph of spirit in the form of one man's careful and passionate art, is still possible. We could not ask for more.

Bruce Weigl
University Park, Pennsylvania
1993

As all historians know, the past is a great darkness, and filled with echoes. Voices may reach us from it, but what they say to us is imbued with the obscurity of the matrix out of which they come; and try as we might, we cannot always decipher them precisely . . .

Margaret Atwood
The Handmaid's Tale

GREETINGS!

Greetings!

Lastname firstname middlenamelast
Bendover and spreadyourcheeks
Mumps/chickenpox/heartmurmur/flatfeet/brokenbones/asthma/badback/mentalillness
Takeonestepforward repeatafterme
Welcome RA17725323*
Getyourfaggotassoffmybus andoutofmystreet andoffmygrass andintomybarracks
Dropyourcocks and grabyoursocks
Thereareonlytwokindsofpeopleinthisman'sArmy thefucker and thefuckee
Ifitmoves saluteit ifitdoesn'tmove paintit
Don'tcallmesir Iworkforaliving
Iamalawnmower and yourassismygrass
Yourmilitaryleft meatheads
Ineededmen but theysentmeyoupussies
Dropdown and givemeten
Ican'thearyou
Assumethecockroachposition cockroach
Vietnamain'tmuchofawar but it'stheonlyonewegottoday
Theonlygoodgook is adeadgook
Doyouwantgooks rapingyourmother inMissouri?
Yourmissionis tolocate closewith and destroytheenemy
Smoke'um ifyou got'um
Thisisyourrifle and thisisyourgun oneisforpleasure theother'sforfun
Don'tjerkthetrigger likeitwasyourpud squeezeit likeyourgirlfriend'stit
Nobrassnoammo sir
Longthrust parry and hold
Tokill isthespirit ofthebayonet
IfIdieinacombatzone just boxmeup and shipmehome
Airborne/Ranger/GreenBeret/C.I.B.** nobody'sgonnafuckwithme
IamtheInfantry QueenofBattle Followme . . .

* RA—abbreviation for "Regular Army" or volunteer   ** C.I.B.—Combat Infantryman's Badge, awarded for genuine combat experience only

4

Notification Of Overseas Assignment

After nearly two years of stateside preparation and training,
I knew that orders for Vietnam would probably come any day.
And I was correct.

But my very first notification of overseas assignment
didn't come from my commanding officer,
or even from the Department of the Army.

It came in the form
of a phone call
from a life insurance company.

"Thank you for your interest
in our 'No War Clause' policy,"
the perky young woman said.

"We're sending your wife a handy desk calendar
for her to keep track of your overseas days on.
Goodbye!"

APO 96225

8

L R

Good Training

"Kill." said the Basic Training NCO, "You're here to
learn to kill!"
"Yes, Sergeant," I replied (but I knew that I never would).

"Kill," shouted the hand-to-hand combat expert,
"You've got to want to kill!"
"Yes, sir," I replied (but I knew I never would).

"Kill!" shrieked the rifle range officer, "You must kill
without thinking!"
"Yes, sir." I replied (but I knew I never would).

"Kill!" lectured the combat veteran, "Over here
it's kill or be killed!"
"Yes, Sergeant," I replied (but I knew I never would).

Three days later, as we swept across a rice paddy,
a small figure leapt from a spider hole
right in front of me.

I killed him.

PAVN

9

APO 96225*

A young man once went off to war in a far country,
and when he had time, he wrote home and said,
"Dear Mom, sure rains a lot here."

But his mother—reading between the lines as mothers
       always do—wrote back,
"We're quite concerned. Tell us what it's really like."

And the young man responded,
"Wow! You ought to see the funny monkeys."

To which the mother replied,
"Don't hold back. How is it there?"

And the young man wrote,
"The sunsets here are spectacular!"

In her next letter, the mother pleaded,
"Son, we want you to tell us everything. Everything!"

So the next time he wrote, the young man said,
"Today I killed a man. Yesterday, I helped drop napalm
       on women and children."

And the father wrote right back,
"Please don't write such depressing letters. You're
       upsetting your mother."

So, after a while,
the young man wrote,
"Dear Mom, sure rains here a lot."

11

* APO 96225, Army Post Office Number 96225
  —Official address of the 25th Infantry Division in Vietnam

12

The Weather Of Vietnam

There are two kinds of weather in South Vietnam:
Hot and dry,
and hot and wet.

During the hot and dry,
the dust is as fine as talcum powder,
and hangs like a gritty mist in the air.

During the hot and wet,
the monsoon wind blows so hard
that it rains sideways.

14

Nui Ba Den

In the central highlands of Vietnam
the mountain of Nui Ba Den
rises three thousand feet into the clouds
from the jungle floor near Tay Ninh.

Once, in the distant past,
a mourning woman named Den
climbed the peak and committed suicide
as close to heaven as possible.

Den's husband died as a soldier
and she hoped the gods would
allow her to join him quickly
and would act to prevent further wars.

But Den's final resting place
is of strategic importance in the area
and for centuries, enemies of the Vietnamese
have fought for control of it.

Chinese, Japanese, French and Americans
have died by the thousands on the mountain's slope
and Ba Den's ancient sacrifice is lost
among the international bloodstains on its summit.

16

Man Of God

The Chaplain of the 25th Aviation Battalion at Cu Chi
prays for the souls of the enemy on Sunday mornings,
and earns flight pay as a helicopter door gunner
during the rest of the week.

LNS

Papasan

You question me with ancient eyes
that have never known peace.
And I answer with young eyes
that do not understand this war.

Killin'

Ira Jeeter was a mean little son-of-a-bitch
always had been, too
A gimlet-eyed Ozark hillbilly
who really got off on
killin'
with rocks, beetles and toads and turtles and snakes
And later
killin'
with slingshots, birds and cats and squirrels and rabbits
And then
killin'
with guns, dogs and quails and geese and deer and coons
In truth
Ira never really felt alive
lessen' he was doing some
killin'
like butcherin' hogs
or quarterin' cows
or his favorite kind of killin',
poppin' the heads clean off live chickens
Ira always got a big hard-on from that type of
killin'.

Ira loved
killin'
like his kinfolk loved
Sweet Jesus
and when the County Judge
let Ira join the Marines
instead of goin' up the river for tryin' some
people
killin'

Ira found
killin'
Heaven
The Marines also loved
killin'
they talked all the time about
killin'
They yelled a lot about
killin'
They sang hymns about
killin'
They even prayed about
killin'

20

The Marines and Ira felt it was a sacrament
killin'
The Highest Calling
killin'
God Bless America and Apple Pie and Joe Dimaggio and
killin'.

So the Marines gave Ira their most favorite tool for
killin'
A brand new oil-smelling brown and black
long-barreled rifle with a ten-power scope
just perfect for
killin'
The Marines trained Ira for months to be good at snipor
killin'
And the Marines sent Ira to Vietnam and placed him
on a green hilltop overlooking a
Free Fire Zone
just full of enemies that needed
killin'
and Ira got a target in his sights right off
a young farmgirl walking to school
and he drew a perfect bead on her tiny left breast
and trembling
began to gently stroke the hairbreadth trigger
for his very first
human
killin'—

When
for the only time in his life,
something soft touched his heart
He hesitated
and instead of killin',
sat up and grinned.

An instant later
Ira Jeeter lay flat on his back,
turned off like a light switch
by one clean bullet behind the ear
fired by a quiet French teacher from Haiphong
who'd always
hated
killin'.

S.O.P.*

To build a "gook stretcher," all you need is
two helicopters,
two long, strong ropes,
and one elastic gook.

* S.O.P., military jargon for Standard Operating Procedure

24

A Conversation On A Sunny Afternoon Near Go Dau Ha

"See, what'd I tell ya? They ain't laughin' now, are they?"

"No. No, they're not."

"And who gives a shit? Nobody, that's who."

"Me. Me, *I* give a shit."

"No, you don't, Lieutenant. No, you don't."

"Yes, yes I do . . . "

"No, you don't. You didn't *do* anything, did you?"

"But what could I have done? What?"

"You could have called battalion."

"Yes."

"You could have run over and joined them."

"Yes."

"Or you could even have shot me!"

"Yes."

"But you didn't—because you don't really give a shit either."

Lieutenant Hatfield

Lieutenant Hatfield figured that he was a survivor.
One night, a mortar round shredded the mosquito netting over his hammock,
but he escaped completely unscathed.
A couple months later, a single 50cal round
went right through the top of his steel pot
without touching a hair on his head.
Another time, he stepped on a "Bouncing Betty"*
but only the guys in front and back of him got hit.

Lieutenant Hatfield figured that he was a survivor.
But once, he ordered a trooper from Alabama
to take down the Confederate flag flying over his bunker.
A few weeks later, he wrote up an "Article 15"**
on a soldier he found sleeping on guard duty.
And one evening,
he sent a reluctant patrol into "Indian Country"***
where they got badly ambushed.

Lieutenant Hatfield figured that he was a survivor.
But he didn't survive
the high-explosive fragmentation grenade
rolled under his cot late one night
by his own men.
"He was a survivor, a brave soldier,"
wrote the colonel to Lieutenant Hatfield's parents,
"and he died in a manner you and the nation can be extremely proud of!"

27

* "Bouncing Betty"—a powerful booby trap that jumps into the air waist-high before exploding

** "Article 15"—a written non-judicial punishment which becomes part of a soldier's permanent record

*** "Indian Country"—an area known to harbor dangerous enemy guerillas

28

A Sunday Afternoon Pickup Game

A Sunday afternoon
pickup game,
just ten guys
taking a break from the war.

Nobody seemed to mind
the crooked, homemade net,
the thick dust,
or the heat.

Overtime! A tie game,
and in the excitement
of trying for another point,
killing was forgotten.

But before we could
finish the game,
a lone mortar round
wiped out half the players.

The final score
for the day:
The VC—5.
The U.S.—0.

Interrogation

What do you say
to an 11-year-old Vietnamese guerilla
who asks,
"What did I ever do to you?"

L R

32

"Good Morning, Vietnam!"

"Good morning, Vietnam!" was our daily wake-up call,
if we weren't too far out in the boonies or weren't in the middle of an ambush
or in a drug-induced stupor.
Every day for 365 days
we awoke to AFVN*.

And after a while,
it didn't seem incongruous anymore to hear the corny jokes or banal DJ banter
or "The Army's Official Policy on VD" or the ludicrously-inflated body count reports.
Every day for 365 days
it actually became a kind of comforting routine.

Never mind that the generals wouldn't let them play
the Beatles or The Doors or Country Joe & The Fish or Crosby-Stills-Nash and Young
or Dylan or Baez. Because
every day for 365 days,
8-track tapes of anti war music arrived by the thousands in the mail from the states.

And besides, Hanoi Hannah** was always on the other station, with protest songs like
"I'm Fixin' To Die Rag," "Four Dead In Ohio," "Stop! Hey! What's That Sound?"
and "The Unknown Soldier."
Every day for 365 days,
those lyrics rocked through our hearts and minds with an almost murderous rhythm.

In fact, I remember one time that a fire-fight broke out right in the middle of
Peter, Paul and Mary's "Where Have All The Flowers Gone?"
The 50cal gunner on one of the APC's***
just cranked up the volume on his transistor tape player as loud as it would go,
and started poppin' off rounds right in time with the beat of the song.

   * AFVN—Armed Forces Vietnam Network
  ** Hanoi Hannah—a North Vietnamese radio peace and propaganda disc jockey
 *** APC—Armored Personnel Carrier

Tet Attack

On the evening of the second day of Tet,* 1968, at Bien Hoa,
a 122mm rocket landed just outside the air base perimeter
sending the GI's and nurses and hootch maids scrambling for cover.

A few minutes later, the second rocket (with a time-delay fuse)
exploded deep inside a large cesspool
splattering Kotex, pink toilet paper, rubbers and sewage
all over the place.

Within five days, the nine soldiers killed by the third and last rocket
had been shipped home and buried and put out of mind.
And their replacements were already working on the flight line.
But three weeks later you could still smell the shit.

* Tet—the annual Lunar New Year Festival

** hootch maids—Vietnamese women hired to clean GI barracks and tents

For Cissy Shellabarger, R.N., Wherever You Are

Tet-stunned
and very nearly scalped
by a hundred razored fragments
from a Chicom* 122mm rocket,
my unconscious carcass
was hastily carted to the Cu Chi hospital
and added to the long line
already there and awaiting attention.

An anguished and blood-sotted doctor
too weary and rushed and young
for what he'd already been conscripted to do,
glanced at my cranial lacerations,
shook his head sadly,
and went on to the next American teenager,
who obviously had a far better
"survival probability."

But an Army nurse (someone told me later)
just as weary and rushed and young
had already seen enough of death that night
and simply decided to buck the odds one time.
"Nobody croaks on Cissy!" she warned both me and God

And she was right.
I didn't die.
In fact, I suspect the more grievous wounds were hers.

* Chicom—GI abbreviation for Chinese Communist

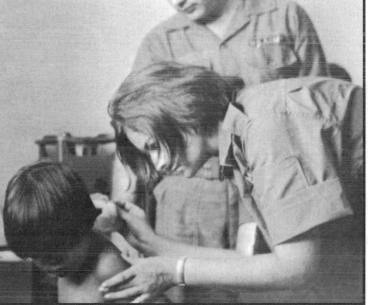

US ARMY

No "Form Letter Format" Available

"Hey, Sarge!
What do I put in this letter?
I mean, I can't tell the Captain's parents
that their only son was killed
while flying his chopper to Saigon
to get some nutmeg for the General's Mess,*
right?"

* General's Mess—special dining room for field grade officers and invited guests

What Kind Of War

What kind of war is this
where you can be pinned down
all day in a muddy rice paddy
while your buddies are being shot
and a close-support Phantom jet
which has been napalming the enemy
wraps itself around a tree and explodes
and you cheer inside?

Day 365

They sit silently
long accustomed to silent waiting.
The only movement comes from sun-burned skin
irritated by freshly starched khaki.

Quiet.
Yet each line of each face tells of pain, violence,
    and sudden death.
The time is soon but habit keeps every man tense,
    alert, tingling.

It's heard before it comes into sight
sliding down over small huts at the runway's far end.
The distant clatter of small arms brings the men
      to their feet,
empty hands clutching yesterday's weapons.

Then all eyes watch the landing
as the rear wheels bounce once, twice, finally settle.
Soon the nose gear is down, too,
and the men cheer, and dance, and crowd against
      the velvet rope.

Slowly, the engine whine fades, and the cabin door
      pops open.
The men whistle and call to the tired and rumpled
      stewardess
who smiles back painfully
as the steps are wheeled up.

Then a long pale line descends the stairs
and files slowly across the black asphalt.
The waiting men now surge through the gate,
      shouting, and
self-consciously ignoring the new group.

For the arrivals, the trip has just begun.
They look questioningly at the pressing throng but
no words are necessary.
The weary bodies and empty eyes tell too much.

Then the lines have passed, and the veterans push aboard
the air-conditioned plane, scrambling for window seats,
playing grab-ass.
And many laugh for the first time in a year.

The flight home is much longer than the one over.
Conversations end in mid-sentence; card games die
      from lack of concentration.
The men eat cold cheese sandwiches, and avoid
      one another's eyes.
And no one speaks of the 223 plastic body bags
      in the cargo hold just beneath their feet.

Thirty-seven hours later the Golden Gate appears
      out of the clouds below.
The men all crowd to the windows.
Some just stare.
Others cry, and are not ashamed.

IN THE LONG SLEEPLESS WATCHES OF THE NIGHT

46

Where Are You, Norman Rockwell?

America.

I dreamed every night for a year about America.
But when I got back, it wasn't here anymore.

America.

In The Long Sleepless Watches Of The Night

When the midnight ghosts rise up
to choke me with old fears,
to gorge me on yesterday's terrors,
to rekindle that latent shallow rage—

I spring from my bed,
rush downstairs to my office,
grab a fully-loaded pen,
and launch an immediate counterattack

of rhyme, meter,
hyperbole, imagery,
metaphor, connections
and symbolism.

The words words words
repulse the demons,
and rise like a bunker of sandbags
to shelter my besieged sanity.

Hours later, the assault repelled,
I stumble back to my pillow
exhausted from the fight,
and collapse.

Yet even as my eyes close,
and my body surrenders at last to sleep,
around the perimeter of my newly-reinforced defenses
I can feel the old enemies regrouping.

50

Cocktail Chatter And Wineglass Laughter

What was it like, you ask? Well, I'll tell you what.
Forget body counts, Free Fire Zones, and winning hearts and minds.
Talk to me instead with smooth sarcasm and textbook irony
about shit that really doesn't matter at all.

52

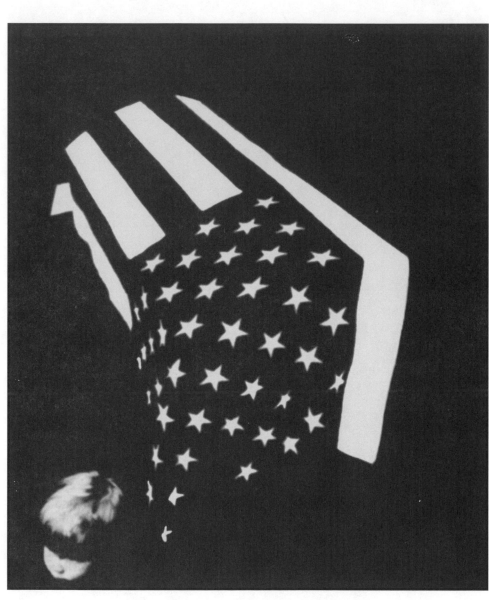

Postmortem

The coffins, draped with American flags, were rolled
one-at-a-time to a column formed in front of the families,
while an Army drummer beat out a slow cadence on a
crepe-covered snare drum.

          —THE BOSTON GLOBE

Line up silently, Manchester, New Hampshire.
Line up silently in front of the
five flag-draped coffins.

Silent ashamed mourning.
Like the silent ashamed acquiescence
when you let them take your sons away to war.

Vietnamese parents cry and wail when their sons go,
and when they die.
Could that mean they love their sons more?

Line up silently, Manchester, New Hampshire.
Line up silently in front of the five boys
your silence killed.

U S   A R M Y

The Policy About Children

I still haven't got it straight . . .
the policy about
children.

Our Geneva Convention Card made it clear
"Try not to harm civilians, particularly the elderly, women and
children."

But combat-wise NCO's preached otherwise,
"Gooks have no respect for human life. They'll attack you with their own
children!"

And calloused short-timers called it a "Double Header"—
Zappin' a pregnant woman; eliminating a breeder of Viet Cong
children.

If I had to fight, I wanted to do it toe-to-toe, man-to-man
but most of the enemy faces I saw were those of
children.

Smiling, running, swimming, playing, singing, joking, laughing,
sleeping, fishing, weeping, hiding, watching
children.

We gave them gifts in exchange for their freedom.
We slaughtered their parents while we played with
children.

We built them schools and playgrounds and showers and swimming pools
and wanted desperately to be loved by the
children.

And we grieved as if for our own
when we accidently or deliberately killed
children.

The politics and protests back home didn't affect us nearly as much
as those tiny graves dug by the mothers of
children.

I still haven't got it straight . . .
the policy about
children.

Driving Along Interstate 44

I couldn't tell your age exactly,
probably 11 or 12.
But I remember your face.
More than any other.

I remember eyes that had seen only war,
a nose never free from the smell of death,
and a mouth that had never really
smiled.

You watched, expressionless,
each time we convoyed past.
Just another small girl's face
in the faceless throng.

But I came to fear your gaze
more than snipers,
or booby traps.
Their hate is mindless.

Now, 25 years and 12,000 miles from your village—
driving through the blackness of Illinois and Missouri—
I often see you out there, watching.
And I just can't understand why America doesn't see you too!

HARMON
POLSTON ERNEST
POLT ERWIN
POLUSNEY JAMES
POLZIN HENRY
POMERINKE RICHARD
POMERLEAU JAMES
POMEROY ALEXANDER
POMEROY JACK
POWELL RAYMOND
POWELL REGINALD
POWELL RICHARD
POWELL RICHARD
RICHARD W
POWELL ROBERT
POWELL ROBERT ALLAN
POWELL ROBERT ALLEN
POWELL ROBERT CLYDE
POWELL RONALD
POWELL RUSSELL
POWELL SAMUEL
POWELL STEPHEN
POWELL STEVEN
POWELL THOMAS
POWELL TONY
PONCE PAUL
For Sammy
With all my love

SEAOP

The Vietnam Veterans Memorial

"Hush, it's like a church,"
a camo-clad father admonishes his toddler—

"All those names, my God, all those names,"
weeps a Gold Star mother—

"He's right over there, on the 17th panel,"
the volunteer vet guide advises a visitor—

"It's the most popular memorial in the entire nation,"
states *Newsweek* magazine—

"Over 100,000 people a week visit this site,"
trumpets the National Park Service—

"Vietnam vet Jeffrey Charles Davis, 36, committed suicide at the memorial today,"
reports the Associated Press—

60

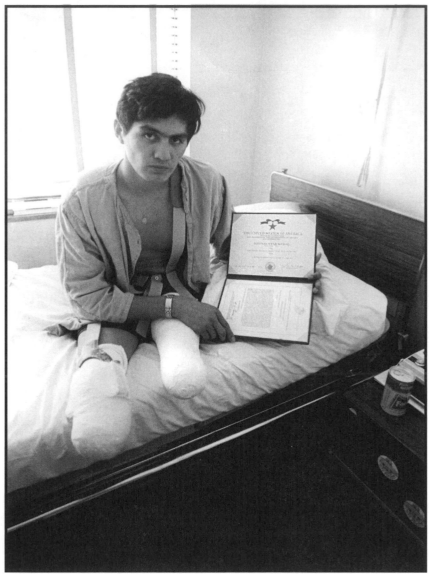

Some Vietnam Vets I Have Known

Peter never made it out of Vietnam.

Neither did George, Ira, Martin, Bill, O.T., Gandy, and so many, many others.

Al disappeared in Mexico about 11 years ago.

Allen and Dave and Stewart and Abel all committed suicide.

Duane deliberately goaded his wife into killing him

(after I refused to do it).

Thomas lives alone in the mountains of Idaho.

Joe has become an avowed communist and works somewhere in New York City.

Jim and Terry and Ted died of cancer before reaching 30.

Chris is in the Arizona State Pen, doing 15 years for smuggling drugs.

Evan has dropped completely out of sight.

M.T. and David and Michael and John and Robert, and nearly all the others I could name, are divorced.

Basil left the country sometime in 1973. I don't know what happened to him.

Larry died unexpectedly last Spring.

According to historians, the war ended on April 28, 1975.

Yet the casualties continue to pile up, these many years later.

I wonder if there will be a place for all their names on the Wall in Washington, too . . .

62

Vietnam Veterans Against The War
Meet
The Daughters Of The American Revolution

"You're disgraceful, all of you!"
sniffed the pink-haired lady in taffeta.
"How could you do this to the troops?"

"Lady,"
replied a calm and sad-eyed vet,
"We are the troops."

63

VVAW

64

Fame

It was a singular fleeting image,
inadvertently captured on film
by an Australian free-lancer
covering the ritual ground-breaking ceremony
of the new Bach Mai Hospital in Cholon.

There were smiles and handshakes all around,
chrome-plated shovels almost irreverently sullied
by policemen, princes, politicians and priests,
and a local rock band
woefully out of tune.

The lone American advisor, a sun-burned 2nd lieutenant,
stood apart from the other officials,
self-consciously clasping one end of a long red silk ribbon.

He understood nothing of the speeches in Vietnamese,
but this was his "Winning Hearts and Minds"
        assignment for the day.

As the bored and stoned cameraman languidly
panned the distinguished guests,
a black-clad teenager toting an ivory-gripped Colt revolver
dashed suddenly out of the crowd
and shot the surprised U.S. soldier through the left eye.

The pictures were slightly out of focus,
but that only seemed to add to their power.
NBC and CBS bid big bucks for the clip,
but ABC's immediate offer of hard cash and a case
        of Chivas Regal made the sale,
and a Puerto Rican courier hand-carried the film
        back to the states that same night.

Next day, on the early evening news,
2nd Lieutenant Bobby Maloof died in full color
in forty million American living rooms.
Near Harrison, Arkansas, a sawmill worker's wife
called from the kitchen, "Lester, what was that
        just on the TV?"

Her husband, who'd been hiding his eyes
from the shimmering screen with a calloused hand
missing three fingers,
replied,
"Nothing. It weren't nothing."

65

Thanks, Guys.

In a firefight as mean as any wartime combat
six dozen hard-core Detroit cops
exchanged bullets with a lone gunman
cornered behind the counter of a downtown 7-11

A thousand rounds smashed every plate glass window
exploded shelf-after-shelf of canned goods
shattered the upright coolers of Coke and Pepsi and RC Cola
and littered the parking lot and street with hot, smoking shell casings

And when the wary SWAT team—
many of them Vietnam vets
who'd been firing at the demons in their own eyes—
finally closed in on their quarry

All they found was the bullet-riddled body
of a skinny middle-aged black man
who had died with a smile on his face
a crumpled pink slip in his pocket

and a pair of green-taped dog tags* around his neck.

* GI's in Vietnam frequently taped their dog tags to keep them from rattling

68

A Visit To The National Cemetery At Springfield, Missouri

Do the bodies blown to bits on Omaha Beach,
or cut to ribbons at Monte Cassino,
or burned to a crisp on Iwo Jima,
or mangled beyond recognition at Khe Sanh,

Stir uneasily

As the Vietnamese gardener
climbs out of a Volkswagen
slips on Italian jogging shoes
and starts rolling over their graves on a Japanese lawn mower?

On The Highway Near Cedar Creek, Missouri, 1986

The toad
BOY
appeared unexpectedly
out of the darkened woods
JUNGLE
He froze, his steady eyes fixed upon me,
and stood his ground as my pickup truck
APC
bore down upon him.

I might have swerved
or tried to stop,
but I couldn't
WOULDN'T
I didn't even feel a bump
as I squashed him into shapeless pulp
SHAPELESS PULP
and then—just as quickly as it happened—I forgot all about it.
I FORGOT ALL ABOUT IT . . .

THE CHILDREN PLAY HAPPILY. AND NO BOMBS ARE FALLING.

This Time

It is a good trip.
I see old familiar places with more mature eyes.
Things which were inexplicable 20 years ago are now
       quite obvious.
I'm glad to be here
this time.

It is a good trip.
I'm carrying a camera and tape recorder instead of
       grenades and an M-16.
There are no mines or booby traps or snipers or
       punji stakes.
I'm glad to be here
this time.

It is a good trip.
People smile and want to talk, instead of fleeing in fear.
They look me in the eye, man-to-man, woman-to-man.
      Equals.
I'm glad to be here
this time.

It is a good trip.
The days are bright and busy, not endless with
      oppressive heat and sullen boredom.
The nights are clear and tranquil, not filled with
      explosions and screams.
I'm glad to be here
this time.

It is a good trip.
I'm seeing Vietnam, Vietnam, not Vietnam, America.
I couldn't imagine this place at peace before.
I'm glad to be here
this time.

It is a good trip.
I don't see the occasional upraised finger, the flat
      hating eyes.
Don't notice the napalm scars or the missing limbs.
I'm glad to be here
this time.

It is a good trip.
Unless I need answers.
Unless I have more questions. But
I'm glad to be here.
This time.

76

L R

Noise

Whenever I think back about Vietnam
the very first thing I remember
is the constant terrible
noise!
All the time
day or night
in the local villages or big cities
or thick jungles or open rice paddies.
Unnatural sounds.

The crump of mortars; the whistle of bombs;
the clap of artillery; the rattle of small arms;
the clanking of tanks; the squawk of radios;
the crackle of flames; the shouts of men;
the wails of women; the screams of children;
the cries of prayer.

But it's not like that here anymore.
And it's totally astonishing
to be in a Vietnam of peace and quiet.
To hear everywhere not the horrible
din of war,
but natural sounds.

The songs of birds; the grunts of pigs;
the ripple of water; the echo of temple gongs;
the hoofbeats of water buffalo; the lilt of raindrops;
the tinkle of bicycle bells; the peeping of tree frogs;
the jesting of men; the banter of women;
the laughter of children;
the murmurs of prayer.

Night Cruisin' Down The Street Without Joy*

The 1986 Toyota mini-bus rocks through the vast dark
as sharp images appear out of the blackness,
      then disappear:
Tiny roadside stands dimly lit by smoky kerosene lamps;
Buddhist shrines faintly illuminated by glowing joss sticks;**
A young couple side-by-side, hand-in-hand, on bicycles;
Three sleepy-eyed water buffalo;
An old man pulling a hand cart heavily laden with firewood;
A laughing group of musicians walking home from some
      late-night performance.

I rush through the variegated landscape, recording it all
      fragmentarily.
Unlike the hectic pace of the working day,
the long night is calm and measured.
People and their hamlets are at rest.
Animals move slowly, if at all.
But my restless mind fills in the void between images
with dreadful daydreams and *deja vu*
of my first visit here, 20 years ago.

I blow through Tuy Hoa and Van Ninh.
Inch up and down Cu Mong and Deo Ca passes.
It grows late.
I grow mellow.
Even the restless surf of the nearby South China Sea
seems tranquil.
War-damaged buildings, as-yet unfilled bomb craters,
are invisible at night.

My thoughts drift.
I think of peace. Of reconciliation.
Then the bored driver pops in a well-worn GI tape
and Dylan intones,
"All the money you make can't buy back your soul."
It's still a damn good song, Bobby,
but you'll never know the half of it.
Not the half of it.

79

* The Street Without Joy—the French nickname for Highway 1, scene of much fighting   ** joss sticks—stick incense

80

Incident In Hue

I shouldn't have stopped.
I really shouldn't have.
After all, I was already running late,
and it wasn't any of my business.

I often went out early in the day,
partly because the air was cool and the Perfume River
      was beautiful.
And also because I'm a morning person who just couldn't
      lay in bed,
especially not there. Not then.

I saw him walking around for nearly a week
and knew he'd been staying at the foreigner's hotel.
I thought he was another dour Russian
who'd complain about the food and scowl at the children.

I enjoyed the sounds and smells of the slowly-awakening city
as the people arose, prepared meals,
and made ready for the long day's activities.
In the hustle and bustle of daybreak, I felt less conspicuous.

I asked my neighbor, Thuy—who works at the hotel—about him,
and she said he was an American teacher
who was visiting the university.
She also told me he'd been a soldier here twenty years ago.

I didn't take a camera or note pad on my sunrise strolls
because I didn't want to look like a tourist.
I'd breakfast on warm French bread and fresh mangoes
      at the open-air market,
and let the flow of the crowds carry me along.

I didn't plan to stop,
but my feet wouldn't let me continue.
I stood nearby, watching,
as he joked with the children.

I usually ended up in a schoolyard,
surrounded by a crowd of boisterous kids.
We'd play soccer, cards, or cat's cradle
as I'd crack them up with my awkward Vietnamese.

I guess I resented his smile
because I remembered my dead mother's advice
that even the kindest of them
were sometimes terribly cruel.

I saw her that clear, calm morning
at the far edge of an excited group of second-graders,
an angular teenager
with a look in her eyes I couldn't begin to comprehend.

I still don't remember picking up the rock
or throwing it.
And although he obviously saw it coming,
he didn't even try to duck.

I saw her suddenly bend over, and then in a single
         fluid motion,
hurl a small stone in my direction.
It floated in slow motion across the heads of the kids
but I refused to believe it was aimed at me.

I watched, horrified, as the rock hit the American
         on the forehead,
just above the right eye.
He didn't flinch,
or even wipe away the trickle of blood that appeared.

I felt the sharp impact, and the spurt of blood
from my second head wound suffered in Vietnam.
The first injury very nearly killed me.
This one hurt worse.

I was summoned before the Peoples Committee
         that afternoon.
They told me he was a good man,
and a friend of our country.
They expected me to say I was sorry.

I attended a dinner sponsored by the Peoples Committee
         that night.
When my hosts asked about the Band-Aid,
I told them it wasn't anything
important.

82

The Kitemaker

Along the northern bank of the Perfume River in Hue,
down a narrow winding dirt path
framed by coconut palms and red-blooming *hoa giay*,
lies the home of Mr. Nguyen Van Huong, 58, kitemaker.

A bright pink fish in the window catches my eye
and I enter the yard and ask to meet its artist.
I show him a wrinkled photo of myself with a big
    Missouri bass.
He grins appreciatively, and slaps me on the back.
    We talk fishing awhile.

Finally, I thank him and prepare to leave, but he
    takes my hand and leads me upstairs
to his cluttered workshop overlooking the water.
There, he proudly shows me his more ambitious creations:
graceful and colorful birds and fish and dragons and
    butterflies—exquisite all.

We examine each one carefully. He explains how
    they're constructed.
His deeply-veined hands flutter through the air,
    demonstrating how the kites fly.
He shows me the delicate rice paper. The finely-split
    bamboo. The homemade glue.
We drink Bao Loc tea. Then Dalat wine. We smoke
    a couple Heroes.* He takes my measure.

And then, as the day grows dim,
he sends his teenage son into a back room.
The boy returns with a dusty but still sinister-looking kite
    modeled after a jet fighter.
It is over six feet long, silver with yellow stars,
    with a detachable bomb on each wing.

Mr. Nguyen says (somewhat sadly, I think), "It flies
    quite well,
but I've only taken it out once,
sixteen years ago,
because it made the children run away screaming."

83

* Heroes—a popular Vietnamese cigarette

A Visit To Mr. Hoa Minh's Physics Class

At the State School on Le Loi Street
where Pham Van Dong,* Vo Nguyen Giap,** and Ho Chi Minh***
were once enrolled,
I visit Mr. Hoa Minh's 9th grade physics class.

The busy students take a break
to tell me about their studies and their lives.
And then, after about 20 minutes,
the teacher asks me to answer some questions about my country.

I go to the front of the room, steeling myself against the expected queries about
the American bombing of Hanoi—
the U.S. Marines' destruction of Hue—
the massacre at My Lai.

A dozen hands shoot into the air
and I apprehensively pick out one questioner.
"I want to know," she says loudly and clearly,
"about Disneyland!"

* Pham—former Vietnamese president
** Giap—general who commanded all North Vietnamese forces during the war
*** Ho—former revolutionary leader and Vietnam's first Prime Minister

The Weaver

The K'ho people of the remote mountains along the Laotian border
have been weavers for centuries.
Their intricately-designed cotton cloth
contains traditional patterns
reflecting their environment and way of life.

In a small stall at the central market in Dalat,
a dusky-skinned lady displays several tablecloths, door coverings and blankets,
all decorated with brilliant birds, animals, and flowers;
along with a single blue, white and red shawl
which clearly stands out from the rest of the offerings.

On a field of the bluest blue,
horizontal lines of white and red are intersected by dozens of unusual geometric shapes.
Closer inspection reveals what was on the weaver's mind
as she shunted the hand shuttle back and forth in her distant village.
Giant silver birds of prey which laid explosive eggs.

Bill Smith's Fiancée

Mai Van Quynh approaches me shyly at the Saigon Zoo.
"You My?"* she asks.
I nod yes.
"You know Bill Smith?" she inquires,
and produces a faded photo of herself and a baby-faced GI.
Inscribed on the back in an almost childlike scrawl it says, "Aug. '66, Love, Bill."

"We engaged," she proclaims proudly, and shows me a cheap PX** wedding band
with the gold plating nearly all worn away.
"He go states, but promise come back for me,
so I wait."
Her smile is strained,
her tone resigned but hopeful.

We sit together near the Elephant House
and drink warm lemonade.
I don't know what to say,
so I tell her that America is a very big place,
and that I'm sorry,
but I don't know her Bill Smith.

She sips her drink.
Watches me closely.
She is painfully thin
but carries herself well for a woman her age.
"We engaged," she repeats,
"so I wait."

* My—Vietnamese for "American"   ** PX—Post Exchange or military department store

90

On Kham Thien Street

"I thought," says Ngo Thi Han, "that America had gone crazy!"

On December 20, 1972, Operation Linebacker II—
more commonly known as "The Christmas Bombing"—began.
For twelve days and nights, at intervals of every two hours,
hundreds of U.S. warplanes bombed targets in and around Hanoi.
Giant B-52's released individual loads of 30 tons of 500-pound bombs
from an altitude of almost six miles.
F-105's and F-4's strafed the city with 20mm cannons,
and dropped canisters of white phosphorous and napalm and anti-personnel cluster bombs.

"I thought," says Ngo Thi Han, "that America had gone crazy!"

Back in the United States
Nixon interrupted 150 million TV dinners
to explain that he was only attacking "appropriate military targets."
Most people didn't listen
or understand.
And none of the pupils at Kham Thien Elementary School—including Han—
heard the announcement,
because they were buried in the rubble, listening to their classmates die.

"I thought," says Ngo Thi Han, "that America had gone crazy!"

Tale Of The Bot Fish And The Crab

The bot is a tiny fish,
not much bigger than a minnow,
which lives in the shallow waters
of the South China Sea.

The bot appears small
and harmless,
so the much larger and more aggressive red crab
often tries to feed on it.

The crab leaps upon
the slow-moving bot,
and grabs it
by the tail.

But the little bot
is very strong,
and it squirms and shakes violently,
sometimes for hours.

Eventually,
the struggle breaks off the attacker's claws,
and the helpless crab
is consumed by the bot.

It's an ancient tale,
and absolutely true.
One they don't teach
at West Point.

94

Four-Star Mother

She squats uncertainly in the doorway of her tiny house
squinting at the ex-GI
who's come from halfway around the world
and two decades in the past
for this Hanoi-sanctioned visit.

Over tea and fruit
she watches with 70-year-old clear eyes
and listens with still-sharp ears
to the uncomfortable statements
and awkward translations.

But after all the talking,
she has only one question.
"Are you the one,"
she asks,
"Who killed my four sons?"

Homeless Veteran In Hanoi

Go away.
Don't look at me.
Don't talk to me.
Don't take my photograph.

How can everyone
be so happy
and busy,
while the war still rages on in my heart?

Go away.
Don't look at me.
Don't talk to me.
Don't take my photograph.

98

The Hanoi Poets Know All Their Poems By Heart

The Hanoi poets know all their poems by heart.
They stand up to recite,
their joss stick eyes
focused upon the moment.

I have enough bad memories to last a thousand years,
says Cao Tien Le.

The Hanoi poets know all their poems by heart.
Their words drown out the whispered conversations,
the squeaking overhead fans,
the clamor of horns from the busy street outside the open window.

Dear American Mothers:
We hear your cries for your soldier sons,
and we do not need translations to tell us of your sorrow,
for we recognize in ourselves the same grief,
says Xuan Thieu.

The Hanoi poets know all their poems by heart.
The spirits they conjure up
ride tendrils of cigarette smoke
to the ceilinged heaven above.

There are still dangerous, unexploded mines in the harbors
and bombs in the forests. And there are also still explosives
in the hearts and minds of both our peoples,
especially for veterans and their families,
says Huu Thinh.

The Hanoi poets know all their poems by heart.
They tell their stories with their faces.
And their hands.
And their lives.

By 1963, even our mothers' lullabies were about war,
says Pham Tien Duat.

At age 8, my daughter wrote a poem asking why America
wanted to kill flowers, trees, crickets, and children,
says Pham Ho.

The Hanoi poets know all their poems by heart.
And they roll on and on,
unfazed by microphone failure
or the loss of electric lights.

I don't understand American GI's. In my writing,
I describe them as extensions of their fighting machines.
I never knew any Americans, so it was easy
to describe them as non-human,
says Xuan Thieu.

The Hanoi poets know all their poems by heart.
And they keep on performing,
even after the program is over,
even after the audience has departed.

Politics—like poetry—is elliptical and subtle.
It takes years to master,
and generally goes unappreciated,
says Nguyen Co Thach.

The Hanoi poets know all their poems by heart.
And they jostle out of the hall, still reciting;
Amble arm-in-arm down the sidewalk, still reciting;
Disappear into the darkness, still reciting.

The cup of love is hotter than the cup of vodka,
says Le Luu.

Come, let's exchange words, not bullets,
says Ho Phuong.

Let's have some fruit and drink and conversation,
and talk no more of war,
says Vo Nguyen Giap.

Waterbugs

You only see them by the bright sunshine of day in old Saigon.
Someone (the government? the police?) keeps them away from the tourists downtown.

Lying or strapped on boards with tiny wheels,
they beg silently for rice, water, or a few dong.*

Twisted, partially paralyzed, limbs missing, wrapped in tattered cocoons of rags,
they scoot about the busy streets in starts and stops.

Pedestrians, bicycles and motorbikes flow around them unimpeded.
Dogs bark at them. Children shy away.

Who are they? Where are their families? How do they bathe or go to the toilet?
Where do they go at night?

You don't see them unless you look.
But the closer you look, the more you see.

The Vietnamese call them *tan phe* (the deformed ones),
and don't like to talk about them at all.

* dong—Vietnamese currency

102

Doi Moi*

In Vietnam,
we have an ancient proverb:
"When you open the door to admit fresh air,
you also let in the dirt."

103

* Doi Moi—"economic renovation" which encourages foreign investment, particularly American

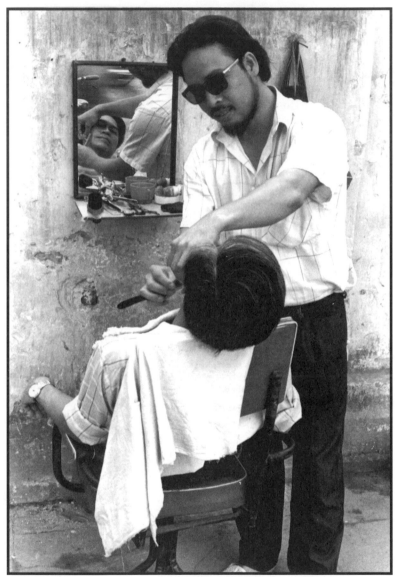

Haircut In Haiphong

The shop is just a chair and a chipped mirror
set against a wall on the sidewalk near the market.
The barber is a muscular older man with sharp dark eyes
behind round, steel-rimmed spectacles.

With ancient scissors, he snips crisply at my thinning hair,
and confides in me that he is a former NVA colonel.
In a halting conversation of Vietnamese, French and English,
he tells me the story of his wartime years.

"I was at the front when I first learned the terrible news,"
he says while vigorously lathering my beard with a scratchy pig bristle brush.
"American bombs fell on my house,
and all of my family was killed at once."

His steady hand trembles momentarily,
as it holds a well-worn razor at the throat of his former enemy.
I turn to look at him directly,
and see a face clouded with memories and tears.

He leans forward, and his strong brown fingers clutch my shoulders.
"Were we all crazy?" he asks. "Were we all crazy?"

The haircut and shave are well done,
and cost only 500 dong.*

* 500 dong equal approximately five cents

Fifth Daughter

Don't be angry that I talk of hard matters,
but I haven't spoken to an American since 1973,
and I have many questions to ask.

I am the fifth daughter in a family of nine children.
My last sister was only just born
when GI's killed her and my mother.

Please forgive my personal questions,
but why did you come to my small country
to make war on us in our own homes?

My father told us when we were little that Americans were good,
that your nation was very big and very rich,
and that you were coming to Vietnam to help us.

I am sorry that I cannot speak without these many tears,
but my memories are so pitiful
that I cannot help myself.

You destroyed my city and my youthful years,
and I may never get the chance for asking again.
So—what do you tell your own children about the war?

"What Did You Do In Vietnam, Daddy?"

Sandbags.
That's what I did,
sandbags.
Hundreds. Thousands. Tens of thousands of
sandbags.

We filled them constantly.
Day and night.
While we smoked and told lies and listened to music.
While we took turns sleeping and eating and crapping.
And sometimes even while we fought.
Sandbags.
Crinkly pale green plastic baggies reinforced with tough nylon thread.
We filled them with sand and mud and rocks.
We used entrenching tools and steel pots and hands.
Sandbags.
We built walls and tunnels and bunkers and houses out of
sandbags.
We constructed walkways and bridges and helipads and latrines out of
sandbags.
We papered and paved the whole goddamned country with
sandbags.
Many times over.
But no matter how hard or fast we worked filling
sandbags,
we couldn't begin to keep up with the rain and rot.
Sandbags.

Son, that's what I did in Vietnam.
Sandbags.

U S A R M Y

L R

A Visit To The Ho Chi Minh City Amerasian* Children's Center

"Hello! How are you? How do you find my country? Are you my father?"
"Hello! How are you? How do you find my country? Are you my father?"
"Hello! How are you? How do you find my country? Are you my father?"

* Amerasian—known in Vietnam as *mau ngoai xam*, or "carriers of foreign aggressor blood"

A Conversation With General Tran Van Tra*

As a veteran and writer
just tell the truth about Vietnam.

Think of it
as your last mission of the war.

As soldiers, we were architects of death.
But as poets, we are engineers of the soul.

* Tra—former commander of all guerilla forces in South Vietnam

114

A Conversation With Miss Ngo Thi Phuong Thien

You ask what I think about you.
I do not think about you.
I am not here for you.
I am a daughter of Vietnam.

China Beach

The waves on China Beach advance and retreat
with an agenda uniquely their own.
The tides here are more accurate than American watches,
more punctual than French ministers,
more eternal than Japanese calendars,
more predictable than Chinese invaders.

The waves on China Beach advance and retreat
the way wartime memories ebb and eddy
around the obstructions of my daily routine back home,
repeating over and over the gentle whisper of Ho Chi Minh:
"The wheel of life turns without pause . . .
Men and animals rise up reborn."

The waves on China Beach advance and retreat,
and I kneel upon the forgiving sand
and surrender the grief
I've hoarded
for
20 years.

Reconciliation

I wanted my return trip to be a positive experience,
and I planned to share what I learned with my community.
But another major reason for my going
was the selfish desire to put some personal ghosts to rest.

I've been too busy since I got back
to examine whether or not I've gained any valuable new perspectives.
But last night, for the first time ever,
I had a dream about Vietnam at peace.

The Children Play Happily. And No Bombs Are Falling.

My friend Chi Tinh Do
who fled his country 18 years ago
wants to know what Vietnam is like today.

And I reply:
The children play happily.
And no bombs are falling.

But Do asks,
What about the re-education camps?
Where are the Catholic nuns?

And I reply:
The children play happily.
And no bombs are falling.

But
What about Freedom of the Press?
Can people come and go as they please?

And I reply:
The children play happily.
And no bombs are falling.

But
Why isn't there enough medicine?
Why do bananas cost more than steel?

And I reply:
The children play happily.
And no bombs are falling.

But
You don't understand.
You're not Vietnamese!

And I reply:
The children play happily.
And no bombs are falling.

VOICES FROM THE HO CHI MINH TRAIL

Trung Tuong Vo Bam* Gets A New Assignment From Uncle Ho In 1959

"Comrade Vo,
build me a supply road by hand from Hanoi to Saigon,
with five main North-South routes
and twenty-one East-West branches.
Even though it will be an elephant-sized project,
keep it secret and hidden.
And when it's complete,
report back to me."

* Vo Bam—the North Vietnamese Army officer who designed,
supervised the construction of, and managed the operations
of the Ho Chi Minh Trail

A Vanguard Youth

At the age of ten,
everyone in our school
became a Vanguard Youth
on the Truong Son Strategic Supply Route.*

One of the East-West routes
passed by our village,
and all of my classmates
helped out on weekends and vacations.

We were too small
for heavy lifting or construction,
so we cut bamboo for bridges
or carried gravel in baskets.

On special holidays
we'd perform dramas,
play music,
and sing for the fighters

After bad battles
there were many wounded comrades.
Sometimes we became very sad,
but the teachers said we were too old to cry

HKD

* Truong Son Strategic Supply Route—the vast network of roads and trails which the North Vietnamese and Viet Cong soldiers used to transport goods and supplies from the north to the south. It was named after the mountain range which straddles most of the western border of Vietnam with Laos and Cambodia, but American GI's nicknamed the route the "Ho Chi Minh Trail." And the media used this term so pervasively, that eventually many Vietnamese began to use it themselves

The Ben Hai Bridge

Under orders from General Vo,
we built an elaborate bamboo bridge
in plain sight
over the Ben Hai River.

We placed the span
in a narrow, winding canyon
between two high mountains,
so it would be difficult to bomb.

Every day,
the American planes would attack it.
Every night,
we would repair it.

There were 12.7mm, 23mm, and 57mm
anti-aircraft gun emplacements
all around the bridge.
In six years, we shot down seventeen planes.

And during all that time,
trucks, bicycles, porters, and fighters
crossed the river safely
on a camouflaged bridge one half mile downstream.

129

P A V N

130

Cao Tien Le's Most Terrible Memory

I was a young officer in my first command,
leading a long column of brand new recruits who were moving South.
We'd only been on the trail for two days,
when an American airplane attacked us.
The narrow path was cut into a mountainside,
so there was no place to hide.
A bomb fell right behind me, and knocked loose a huge boulder
which fell on top of three boys.

The rock squashed them so completely
that only their heads stuck out from under it.
Yet somehow, they hadn't been killed.
"Help, help!" they pleaded pitifully.
I knew that the pilot would report our position,
and that more planes would come soon.
We had to move on quickly,
but I couldn't decide what to do.

The boys were gagging and rolling their eyes.
I couldn't let them suffer,
and I knew what would happen to my untested troop's morale
if every one of them had to step over those horrible heads.
So I shot each boy twice between the eyes,
and I cut all three heads off at the neck.
I put the heads under some rocks next to the trail, covered the blood with dirt,
and we marched on.

131

132

The Truck Inspector For The 559th Special Unit Of The Peoples Army

I was the safety inspector
for trucks traveling the trail.
The rough roads and heavy loads were bad,
but the worst damage
was done by bullets of strafing planes
and shrapnel from B-52 bombs.

Trucks would return from the South
with fenders missing,
windshields shattered,
radiators leaking,
headlights broken,
tires shredded.

The drivers used
wire,
rope,
vines,
bamboo,
and tree sap to make emergency repairs.

Some trucks were so shot up
you could see right through them.
One day, Party cadres ordered me
to start counting the holes.
Any truck with over fifty
should be removed from duty.

The next morning,
a convoy of three dozen vehicles
arrived at my checkpoint.
The first truck had over 100 holes in it,
and some of the others had even more.
After that, we didn't count holes any more.

PAVN

134

The Butterfly Painter

Before the American War
I was an art teacher at Nam Dinh Middle School.
In 1962, I volunteered to work on the trail,
and they made me a sign painter.

The Party gave me patriotic slogans to write,
like:
"Let the road wait for vehicles;
Never the vehicles for the road."

And: "Walk without footprint;
Cook without smoke;
Speak without sound;
Arrive without image and leave without silhouette."

They were good sayings,
but I always added my own signature, too.
A small brightly-colored butterfly.
They couldn't replace the real ones destroyed by war, but I think they helped.

136

A Village Water Well

For six centuries, our village had the only reliable well
    in the area.
So when the Peoples Army built the trail,
they made it pass nearby.

For years, we carried water to the workers, porters,
    and fighters.
And although they had no money to pay us,
they often gave us trinkets or trail scrip.*

Then, in 1967, U.S. Special Forces came to our hamlet.
They erected a big sandbag fort on the soccer field,
and ordered us to bring them free water every day.

Soon, we were taking water to the Americans by day,
and to the Resistance at night.
We got very tired.

After about a year, the Americans discovered what
    we were doing,
and ordered us not to help the Peoples Army any more.
We said we wouldn't, but we lied. We had no choice.

The GI's threatened us, and even beat us.
And one night, they shot my cousin, Thong, who was only
    watering his garden.
It was a very bad time.

Then a new American captain took over.
He spoke Vietnamese quite well,
and he asked the villagers many questions.

He ordered his men to leave our women alone,
and to stop shooting the water buffaloes.
And he also said it was okay to share the well water
    with whoever needed it.

Unfortunately, the good captain was killed in battle
    with the V.C.,
and his replacement blamed our people.
So the U.S. soldiers burned down our village,
    poisoned the well, and then left.

In 1975, we returned to the village, and rebuilt
    the houses and shops.
The well is pure and cold again.
And we still provide water for anyone who passes by . . .
    even Americans.

137

* trail scrip—paper currency issued by the Hanoi government which would be honored by merchants and businessmen sympathetic to the liberation struggle

The Orchid Lady

I lived near the trail
but I was too old for construction or carrying.
I used to take the workers water and fruit
when my rheumatism wasn't too bad.
And sometimes I gave flowers to the soldiers.

By 1965, the American chemicals
had killed all the flowers along the road.
So I had the old ladies in my village
begin growing
orchids.

We put the flowers in coconut shells
and tied them to trees along the footpaths.
The soldiers would stop to smell the blossoms,
would remark on their beauty,
and then march on, revitalized.

The Ho Chi Minh Bird

They said I was too old for battle.
Too frail for heavy work.
But I could whistle bird calls,
so they sent me down the trail
to be a Ho Chi Minh bird.

The bombs and chemicals
had killed or frightened off all the birds
whose notes cheered the soldiers.
So, I'd hide in the forest as convoys passed,
and sing all the happy songs I knew.

I started whistling in 1962,
and by the Liberation
I was 257 different birds.
I got malaria, my hair fell out, and I was wounded four times.
But I was a Ho Chi Minh bird every day for thirteen years.

Parachute Seamstress

During the American War,
I was a seamstress in Dong Ha,
a village near the trail.

Night-after-night for years,
U.S. planes dropped many parachute flares
during air raids.

In the mornings,
I would walk up and down the pathways,
gathering the parachutes from trees and streams.

I used the silk
to make nice shirts and fancy dresses
for holidays and weddings.

When the fighting ended
I couldn't get any more material,
so I had to close my shop.

Now, I'm a rice farmer.
I miss the sewing,
but not the war.

144

A Porter On The Trail

In 1966,
when I started down the trail,
I carried a copy of
The Poems of Walt Whitman
in my rucksack.

I am not a learned man,
and I know only
two poems by heart:
"Kim Van Kieu,"* and
"Song of Myself."

I would read as I walked
from North to South, and back.
I could share "Kieu" with anyone,
but had less opportunity to discuss "Song"
with my comrades.

Still, I drew strength from Whitman's poetry,
and optimism too. He wrote,
"All goes onward and outward . . . " and
"To die is different from what anyone supposed,
and luckier."

I wondered
how a nation
that gave birth to Walt Whitman
could also produce
napalm and Agent Orange.

He wrote,
"This is the grass that grows
wherever the land is and the water is,
This is the common air
that bathes the globe."

One day, near Khe Sanh, we captured a GI.
I was excited, and asked him about
"Song of Myself."
But the American said
he'd never heard of Walt Whitman.

* "Kim Van Kieu"—the classic Vietnamese epic poem of selflessness

Relaxing

The American War lasted so long
that we couldn't keep fighting all the time.

Whenever they could,
the cadres gave us time to relax.

We would read, garden, play sports, or swim.
And if we were lucky, there was sometimes romance.

Life on the trail was hard. Often terrible.
But I have some good memories of it as well.

147

148

12 Years With The Literature And Art Army

I am Pham Tien Duat.
I am a college graduate and poet.
I was on the trail from 1963 to 1975.
I fired eleven shots, but never hit anybody.
I'm glad.
I fought best with words.

H K D

150

The Monk's Story

I was training to be a monk
but they drafted me anyway.
When I refused to be a soldier,
they put me in the special forces.

For over ten years
I took medicine South,
and brought the wounded back North.
It wasn't the Way of Buddha, but it wasn't fighting either.

Once, in the rainy season,
when the trucks couldn't go,
I carried a wounded comrade on my back
for nearly 700 kilometers.

I changed the battle dressing twice a day
and walked as gently as I could.
Yet for five weeks, the blood from the fighter's head wound
ran down my cheeks like tears of red rain.

I carried my fallen comrade
all the way to Hanoi,
even for the last six days
when she was dead.

Folk Song Nurse

I was always very small,
even for a woman.
Yet I was trained as a nurse
to help our wounded fighters return North.

They never complained when rations were short,
or when we ran out of morphine for their pain.
I used to walk alongside the trucks and litters,
trying to cheer the soldiers by singing folk songs.

The stern cadres
reprimanded me constantly, saying,
"Don't violate security!"
"Maintain noise discipline!"

But the songs were good medicine,
and the injured comrades (when they could)
would often sing along.
It was better than listening for the bombs.

VNA

154

NTT

Ballet Of The Mortar Rounds

My name is Madam Nguyen Thi Kim,
and I am a former member
of the Vietnam Song, Dance and Musical Ensemble
from Hanoi.

I was only just out of high school when I was asked to join,
and had lived in the comfortable city all my life.
But my singing and dancing skills were needed
to encourage our fighters in their patriotic resolve.

Our twelve-member troupe traveled along the trail
        constantly for eight years,
giving up to 28 shows per month.
We performed in jungle clearings and in caves,
on mountain tops and in tunnels.

We wore elegant gowns or black peasant ba-ba's,*
recited verses from Bac Ho** or "Kim Van Kieu,"
and sang popular resistance songs like
"Saigon Rising Up," and "Making Clothes for Our Soldiers."

My favorite number was one I created to recognize
the women who carried the heavy 81mm mortar
        ammunition on shoulder poles
from the depots in the North
to our comrades in the South.

Their endless task was a fugue of brutal toil,
but they carried it out with heroics, love and grace.
And in their honor, I called the dance
"Ballet of the Mortar Rounds."

155

* ba-ba's—traditional peasant work clothes
** Bac Ho—"Uncle" Ho Chi Minh

156

HKD

The Brigade Of Lady Trieu*

I am Madam Vu Thi Doan,
and for twelve years
I was the leader of the young women volunteers
of the 609th Brigade.

From 1966 to the reunification of Vietnam,
we were an emergency repair crew
for roads, bridges, ferries, etc.,
along the Truong Son Strategic Supply Route.

Three blows of my whistle
and within 45 minutes all 300 of us would set out at once,
by train or truck or on foot,
for the site of severe damage caused by American aircraft.

Each of us had a knapsack,
a green plastic sheet for raincoat and camouflage,
sandals cut from old truck tires,
and a protective helmet of plaited straw.

In hot or cold, under blazing sun or drenching rain,
while bombs were falling or bullets were flying,
we labored mightily to keep the road open,
to repair broken structures and defuse unexploded bombs.

When U.S. planes attacked us,
we fought back with infantry weapons
and anti-aircraft guns
and songs:

My mind won't be at peace until the traffic can start moving.
My dearest wish is that the road should be finished quickly.
Darling, let us put aside our personal feelings for now.
Once the war is over, we shall be reunited!

Our brigade was a big family,
like the fingers of a hand.
When one was hurt,
all of us felt the pain.

We were subjected to 63 raids by the American air forces,
but successfully finished 108 major tasks.
A woman who worked diligently, fought courageously,
       and showed good morals,
was likely to become a good wife and mother.

* Lady Trieu—a national heroine who many centuries ago
  led an armed insurrection against Chinese occupiers

Long-Haired Soldier

By 1975, I had fought the Americans for half my life.
By the time of the reunification
I'd lived side-by-side with male comrades for fifteen years.

We had traveled together; eaten together;
studied together; prayed together;
fought together; bled together.

They called the men "fighters,"
because that's mostly what they did.
And they fought bravely and well.

They called us women "long-haired soldiers,"
but in addition to battling the enemy,
we had many other duties also.

We carried food and ammunition and weapons.
We built roads and bridges and hospitals.
We sewed clothes and raised crops and cooked meals.

We sang and danced and recited poetry.
We gave birth and tended the wounded.
We taught the children and buried the dead.

Many of us women expected all those years
        of mutual struggle
would result in more gender equality after the war.
But we were wrong.

159

Act Of Valor

We were on the trail in eastern Laos when we first heard about that incredible act of valor.
On November 2, 1965, a brave civilian sat down on the street in the capital city,
poured gasoline on himself, lit it, and burned to death,
in order to protest the war.

The news unnerved us, for although we believed we were making a real sacrifice,
none of us in my unit had that kind of selfless courage.
26 years later, every Vietnamese still remembers that patriot's name.
Norman Morrison.*

* Norman Morrison—an American Quaker who committed suicide outside the Pentagon

161

PAVN

162

L R

Floating Down The Ho Chi Minh Trail

I am from the fishing village of Bai Chay, near Haiphong.
My family has lived in the same house for 302 years.
In 1961, the Party asked my father to donate his boat
    to the liberation struggle,
and to begin smuggling supplies to our comrades fighting
    in the South.

Instead of tending our nets and lines each day,
my father and I sailed our sampan up and down the coast.
We'd load guns and munitions at Do Son, hide them
        under a false deck,
then sail South to deliver the cargo to our friends at night.

It was supposed to be a very dangerous job,
but although we saw American ships and planes nearly
        every day,
we were never shot at or bombed.
I missed my playmates, but Father would make up
        wonderful stories to tell me.

I was only a little girl of nine when we started,
and although my mother was worried,
the cadres said that having me along made us appear
        less suspicious.
They were right, for sometimes the Americans stopped us
        just to give me sweets.

In 1969, my father had a fit, and became too weak
        to run the boat.
So I became the boss, while he smoked and slept.
By then, I had breasts,
and the GI's gave me even more sweets, and sometimes
        money, too.

We continued the boat trips until The Liberation.
Twice we nearly sank in bad storms.
Once we got lost and nearly died of thirst.
In 1973, I had an American baby.

Now I am a waitress at the Bach Dang Hotel.
I have married a disabled soldier who cannot have children,
and we get by with my salary and his government stipend.
My son and younger brothers now have the boat,
        and often bring us fresh fish.

The Locomotive Driver On The Ho Chi Minh Trail

I am Tran Minh Thien,
and I'm the Vice Director of the Saigon Locomotive Enterprise.
During the American War, I was an engine driver
on the Hanoi-Haiphong-Vinh run.

I'd pick up goods wagons
loaded with supplies for our soldiers fighting in the South,
and take them as far
as the Lam River near Vinh.

We couldn't take the trains any farther,
because U.S. bombs had destroyed the big bridge there.
So the wagons would be unloaded
and the materials transferred to boats, carts, bicycles and porters.

For fourteen years, I drove that route.
During the day, American planes attacked the railroad constantly.
But even before the bombs had stopped falling,
workers would begin repairing the roadbed and bridges.

In daytime, we hid the trains in tunnels and under leafy nets.
We parked them on spurs in the forests and in bamboo groves.
We camouflaged the wagons to look like carts or houses or pagodas.
In all the fighting, we never lost an engine.

We drove the trains only at night,
by the illumination of flashlights and kerosene lamps.
Because of the bombing damage to the tracks,
sometimes we could only go five or ten kilometers per hour.

But there was never a night
when our trains didn't move.
We knew our goods were desperately needed by our comrades,
so we railroaders fought the war kilometer-by-kilometer.

The Binh Lang Village Defense Force

I knew we couldn't shoot down jet planes with old rifles,
but that's all we had.

Every day, the men and women of my company mobilized
to fire their weapons at the attacking U.S. aircraft.

As the Americans approached, we filled the sky with streamers of gunfire
and yelled patriotic slogans and brave curses.

In nine years, we suffered 47 dead, and many more wounded.
But we didn't destroy a single airplane.

I knew we couldn't shoot down jet planes with old rifles (and my company knew it too),
but that's all we had.

168

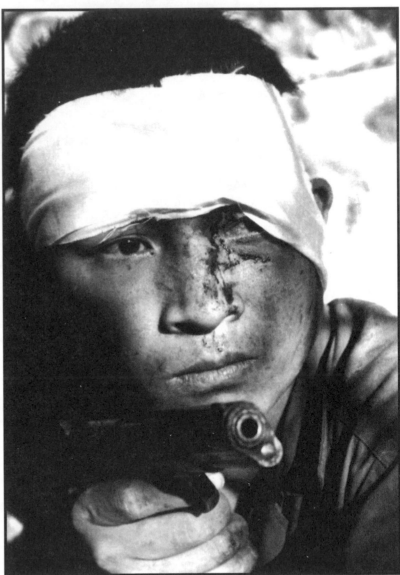

An NVA Sniper From The Siege Of Khe Sanh

Let us speak the truth here.
I killed Americans. A lot of them.
It was my profession. My duty.
You were a soldier too, so I know you understand.

I was best at shooting Marines,
especially when they were eating or taking showers.
I killed Americans,
and I was very good at it.

Diet My—"Destroy the Americans,"
a slogan frequently carved in the trees
along the trail

Soldier Of Information

I am Nha Tho Cam.
From 1968 to 1975, I was the maintenance officer
for the Truc Truong Son
(Ho Chi Minh Trail telegraph system).

We strung a rubber-coated copper cable through the trees
            and bushes
down the entire trail through Vietnam, Laos and Cambodia,
all the way from Hanoi to Loc Ninh.
It took over 3,000 kilometers of wire.

There were one hundred information soldiers,
each of them responsible for thirty kilometers of wire.
They were on duty 24 hours a day,
to repair breaks caused by bombs, artillery, landslides,
            floods and animals.

It was over this crucial wire
that the big generals talked to each other nearly every day.
Vo Nguyen Giap in the North,
and Tran Van Tra in the South.

They transmitted battle orders, agent information,
            and logistical statistics.
Sometimes the Americans found the wire, but listened in
            without understanding.
Because Giap and Tra communicated with each other
in a private code they'd invented as school chums.

H K D

Confessions Of A Hero
Of The Truong Son Strategic Supply Route

In 1971, I was driving a load of valuable munitions
down the trail in eastern Cambodia.
I was in the last truck of a long convoy that had been
      on the road for 78 hours.
I was tired, and during a bad rainstorm I took
      the wrong road, and got stuck.

I tried frantically to dig out, but I couldn't.
So I reluctantly followed standard procedure,
blew up the truck and its cargo,
and made my way on foot back to the base camp.

I was humiliated and scared, but the cadres welcomed me
      with jubilation.
They said that an enemy patrol planning to ambush us
had been distracted and deceived by my truck's location,
and thus my quick actions had saved all my comrades
      and the rest of our materials.

Later, in a big ceremony,
the commander praised my bravery,
and proclaimed me
A Hero Of The Truong Son Strategic Supply Route.

I still have the medal.
My wife keeps it in a teakwood frame on the altar
      to our ancestors.
I'd like to return the award, and tell the true story.
But I don't know how.

Cemetery Architect

I am General Dong Si Nguyen.
I am the designer and builder of the
Truong Son Strategic Supply Route Memorial Cemetery.

Here we honor the memory
of the 42,000 men, women and children
who were killed while building or traveling the trail.

Although over 10,000 people are buried here,
there are only 2,500 headstones
standing on the surface.

I ordered the dead to be buried in four layers
so that visiting civilians during the war
      would not be disheartened
by the excessive number of actual casualties.

Cemetery Superintendent

I'm the superintendent
of the
Truong Son Strategic Supply Route Cemetery.

This forty acres
contains the remains of
over 10,000 men, women and children.

But the actual cemetery
is nearly 16,000 kilometers long,
and stretches from North to South.

So many died,
that you can't stop anywhere along the trail
without standing on a grave.

175

The Victor

My name is Tran Ngoc Khoi.
I joined the Resistance in 1971, and fought on the trail until 1975.
I participated in the liberation of Saigon,
and marched proudly through the streets with my comrades.

Since the war was over
and the Americans had gone,
my days as a soldier were finished
and the cadres told me I could go home.

I had not seen my family in four years,
so I packed my rucksack with some trinkets and toys for them.
But after I got on the train for Da Nang,
I discovered that Saigon pickpockets had stolen all my gifts.

L R

Cyclo Driver

These old legs have gone too many miles.

They hiked the rugged jungle paths of northern Vietnam with Bac Ho in the 40's
They scaled the foggy mountains around Dien Bien Phu with Vo Nguyen Giap in the 50's.
They trudged up and down the tortuous Ho Chi Minh Trail with PAVN in the 60's and 70's.
They hauled cement up the long highway from Haiphong in the post-war 80's.

These old legs have gone too many miles.

They are stiff in the mornings, like sticks.
They make cracking noises like breaking bamboo.
They are too tired to do much work any more.
They should be holding happy grandchildren or resting in the warm sun.

These old legs have gone too many miles.

But now, I pedal tourists from Japan,
France,
and America,
all around the crowded streets of Hanoi

These old legs have gone too many miles.

An Old Porter From The Battle Of Dien Bien Phu*

All the time,
it's Ho Chi Minh Trail this.
And Ho Chi Minh Trail that.
What I want to know,
is how can I get a new motorbike?

* Dien Bien Phu—location of the final battle of the French Indochina War, 1954

BONES

184

A Visit To The Cu Chi* Military District Cemetery

Are you listening, Liet Si?**
Can you hear me?
Feel my footsteps?
Sense my presence?
Fathom my sorrow?

Are you listening, Liet Si?
Here I am
again.
Walking above you
as I did before

Are you listening, Liet Si?
Born underground.
Married underground.
And now buried
underground.

Are you listening, Liet Si?
We fought each other here, on the same day,
23 years ago.
I was wounded.
You were killed.

Are you listening, Liet Si?
As we meet for the first time.
You, finally at rest.
I, still not at peace.
Our chance of becoming friends lost forever.

Are you listening, Liet Si?
To birds, instead of bombs.
To the breeze through pines, instead of battle.
To the laughter of children.
And the murmur of loved-ones' prayers.

Are you listening, Liet Si?
Can you hear me?
I can hear you.

185

* Cu Chi—an area where many of the Liberation Forces
lived and fought in an extensive tunnel system

** Liet Si—fallen soldier

Working Near Hai Van Pass

I was working on the trail
near Hai Van Pass
when the B-52's came.

The bombs killed my brother,
and I buried him
in a field nearby.

The Black Ravens
returned the next day,
and bombs dismembered my brother's corpse.

I picked up
what remains I could,
and re-buried them.

The following day
the planes bombed again,
and obliterated the gravesite.

Before I returned home,
I scavenged the area once more
for pieces of my brother.

I gave our mother what I found.
She still believes she has Tuan's bones,
but it's really only a jar of mud.

The Bone Merchant

He approaches confidently
as I stroll a dense warren of unnamed back streets
behind the Central Market in Ho Chi Minh City.

"Look, look!" he exclaims,
and displays an authentic-looking set of dog tags,
well-worn and burnished as if from years of use.

"M.I.A., M.I.A.," he explains,
and offers a quick glimpse into a musky ammo crate
containing splintered bone fragments.

"You take, only $100 U.S."
It's the old Tu Do Street hustle.
The law of supply and demand.

Our eyes meet, lock, slide away, then lock again,
in recognition of shared terrors twenty years ago
when we were both too young.

"Okay, okay, GI," he says with a knowing shrug.
We stand together awkwardly for a few moments,
shifting our weight from foot-to-foot.

His con is clever and bold, yet totally bogus.
But he knows I could tell him
where too many of his M.I.A. comrades still lie.

I start to speak, but suddenly he's gone.
Disappeared.
The bone merchant.

190

A Farmer From Vinh

"The airplane crashed into my rice paddy on the night of December 21, 1972,"
says the old farmer from Vinh.
"It fell like a star out of the heavens,
and knocked me and my wife right out of our bed!

"The Army soldiers who came running said it was a fighting jet,
and that the driver was still inside.
But after the terrible burning was over,
it looked only like a huge lump of charcoal in my field.

"My wife was afraid of the plane, and wouldn't go near.
But I know its hurting days were finished,
and since the American had no one to say prayers over him,
I built a small altar on the wreckage.

"Each week, I still burn some joss for that young man
who died all alone so far from his ancestors.
Many times the local cadres have ordered me to stop doing that,
but they are all too young to know about important things."

The Bones Of An American M.I.A.
Speak To The Members Of The Joint Casualty Resolution Team

Please, just leave me be.
I'm fine.
I'm not missing.
I know exactly where I am.
Two klicks* northwest of My Tho.
Precisely where the U.S. Army left me.

I've now been resting here
for longer than I lived in Oklahoma.
My blood and flesh and organs and sinews have fused
      with the land.
Bombs and tanks and water buffaloes and wooden hoes
have kneaded me into the earth for over two decades,
until I have become the very soil which nurtures
      the rice and the people.

Please, just leave me be.
I've finally found peace
here in this quiet paddy.
The southeast Asian sun warms me.
Giant cumulus temples of perfect ivory float high overhead.
And the lazy Mekong** bathes me regularly.

I am not alone.
Busy cranes stalk bugs and frogs here.
The great horse snake frequently slides by silently.
Happy children who never saw me in camo fatigues
often fish for the elusive *ca ro**** in the soft glow of dusk.
And at night, ten thousand crickets sing languid lullabies.

Please, just leave me be.
Don't scatter me all about, or scrounge up my bits and pieces
so some bored lab technician in Honolulu can grind me
      into unrecognizable dust,
or some bozo politician can use me—again.
And whatever you do,
don't sell me to H. Ross Perot!

Take the dog tags, if you must.
They belong to the government, but I do not.
You invested me in Vietnam
because you said it was worth my life.
I believed you then. I believe it even more now.
So please, just leave me be.

193

---

* klick—GI slang for kilometer
** The Mekong is Vietnam's largest river, and flows into the South China Sea below Saigon
*** *ca ro*—tiny minnow-like fish that lives in flooded rice paddies

194

A North Vietnamese Veteran Bids Farewell
To The Remains Of An American Pilot In 1989

My name is Tran My Nhuong,
and I'm here to see you off—
back to your own country (where I now have relatives, too).

Who are you? I don't know.
But today you finally return home to your family,
and to an American sky as blue as the sky of Vietnam.

I wish a tranquil heaven for your soul,
gemmed with sparkling stars and a great shining moon.
May you rest undisturbed in your motherland's arms forever.

Face-To-Face With Uncle Ho

Morning shadows still shroud the gray-slabbed mausoleum
located in Ba Dinh Square in downtown Hanoi.
The glass sarcophagus is located deep in the building's interior,
up one flight of smooth marble stairs
worn slightly hollow by thirteen years of endless pilgrims.

Ho reposes upon a bed of plum-colored silk,
dressed in his customary olive-drab military uniform.
The vibrant eyes—even with the lids gently closed—seem to
        directly return my gaze.
Facial lines etched by 79 years of war are still evident,
but the body's attitude reflects an overwhelming sense of final peace.

And there is more in this cold tomb than just Ho's animate corpse
        and silent echoes.
Buddhists believe that the soul hovers above the departed's coffin,
praying for the forgiveness of those who offended the person in life.
Leaving the darkened room, I picture the faintest twitch of a smile,
as if Ho was letting me know that he was aware of my presence.

Outside, in the palm-shaded garden,
a warm winter sun lights the faces of a long line of waiting children.
They are laughing and fidgeting,
a hundred happy sparrows full of life and song.
A whole new generation who have no memories of war, Americans,
        or even Ho Chi Minh.

197

NHN

Song In The Moonlight

You play a tune
and suddenly the light of the moon becomes immense.
The voices of night birds are lost there,
while far above, a melody of stars wanders across the sky.

From the instrument
rise sounds which speak of men, and women, and earth.
Sounds of love of all times past.
Sounds of love today.
All forever waiting in the strings
which endlessly shape the lovely tune.

And all who listen will recognize themselves
in this music's warm human strains.
The young girl who drives a tractor.
The old people who have led so many generations
      to the shores of farewell.
And then the children, so many of them,
who by the song,
suddenly become poets.

And the song vibrates,
and rises in the moonlight
until it seems the strings no longer skim the fingers,
but are stretched into endless space,
like the age-old strength of Vietnam.

And we—the children—we hold our breaths,
we listen with all our ears,
as the shade of the palm tree spreads over the instrument,
passing like a hand
to erase the hateful sounds of war from our hearts.
Leaving only the song,
and it alone,
as fresh as a stream at its source.

199

—**Tran Dang Khoa**
(written in 1972, when he was 17 years old)

AFTERWORD

On Friday, August 13, 1965, I entered the U.S. Army—the result of my local draft board's impatience with the deliberately-leisure pace of my college undergraduate career. I voluntarily opted for Officer Candidate School, thereby extending my military obligation to three years; the first two of which I spent in stateside training, followed by a one-year tour of Vietnam with the 25th Infantry Division in 1967-68.

My experience in the war—which included the largest combat exercise of the conflict, Operation Junction City, and the infamous Vietnamese Tet Offensive of '68—altered my life forever, in ways I still don't fully understand. But I hope this poetry at least partially explains some of the breadth and depth of that wrenching year.

Not only did the terrible memories of the actual fighting remain after I returned home, but also the nagging—and eventually unde-niable—conviction that I had overlooked and/or completely misunderstood the history, culture, and character of the Vietnamese people, for whom the war itself was supposedly being fought.

In my subsequent career as a writer and teacher, I've found that not only do my fellow veterans have the same concerns, but so do a great many non-vets; along with a very sizeable proportion of the children of the Vietnam generation.

So, in order to satisfy my own persistent sense of curiosity, and to be able to answer my students' questions as well, I began to study in earnest about Indochina. I concentrated initially on the accounts of ex-GI's—primarily autobi-ographies, poetry and novels—but found that virtually all such writing also lacked the Vietnamese sensibility I sought. The same was generally true for the major journalists, scholars and politicians who were writing about the war— even those with the more objective viewpoints as representatives of non-combatant nations.

Eventually, I concluded that the answers I sought could only be found in the lives and literature of our former enemies. And since there is very little serious Vietnamese writing about the war (or any other aspect of their society) available in the United States— especially in English translation—I decided that I'd have to return to Southeast Asia, and seek out the accounts of that struggle by the various local participants themselves.

Since 1985, I've been back to Vietnam

(and Laos, Cambodia and Thailand) for nine extensive visits. I've traveled from one end of these countries to the other, by plane, train, car, boat, bicycle and foot. I've visited libraries, schools, archives, military bases, bookstores, newspapers, pagodas and coffee shops.

I've talked with politicians and peasants; businessmen and fishermen; soldiers and veterans; poets and prostitutes; musicians and physicians; teachers and students; monks and thieves; old folks and young children. I've slept in their homes; prepared meals with them; gone to the market with them; gone to their jobs with them; gone fishing with them; attended concerts, plays, movies, poetry readings and soccer games with them; been to weddings and funerals and births with them.

And I've asked everyone I've met—regardless of age—to tell me their story. And they almost always do. Many of these lengthy conversations (some of which last for hours; others which have continued through visits over a period of several years; and others

Fellow Vietnam veterans Nguyen Trong Thanh and Larry Rottmann—who photographed the conflict from opposing sides—hang out in Hanoi, 1992.

which are still ongoing) are the inspiration for the Vietnamese "voices" in this collection—like the Ho Chi Minh Trail accounts by only a few of the over 300,000 military and civilian people who worked on that enormous project between 1959 and 1975.

Here, too, are the remarkable photographs of Nguyen Trong Thanh, who was a reporter on the trail for nine years. Born in Saigon in 1942, Thanh graduated with a degree in History from Hanoi University in 1966. He entered the Peoples Army (of North Vietnam), and following his military training was assigned as a battlefield reporter on the Truong Son Strategic Supply Route—more commonly known as the Ho Chi Minh Trail.

Thanh served in that capacity from 1966 until the national reunification of 1975, observing and photographing hundreds of battles, large and small, including the Tet (Lunar New Year) fighting of 1968 and 1972 in Quang Tri, Hue, Thua Thien, and Danang. He was wounded and received several military decorations during his nine years in combat.

Currently, Thanh is a photo artist and editor for *Vietnam Pictorial* in Hanoi. He is married, with a daughter in college and a son in high school.

Although some of Thanh's photographs were reprinted in Japan, France, Canada and Germany during the war, this collection of his Ho Chi Minh Trail photographs has never been published anywhere before, even in Vietnam.

I hope that this book helps provide some insight into both the American and Vietnamese national character, particularly as it pertains to our long and painful war against one another. And that these poems and photos assist us in realizing that our one-time antagonists are actually much more like us than we ever dared to surmise.

Such mutual recognition appropriately humanizes both our countries, and thus helps to heal the old wounds which have for far too long prevented Americans and Vietnamese from placing the war in the properly-distant personal and historical perspective.

Larry Rottmann
Springfield, Missouri
1993

I'm very pleased to be collaborating with my good friend and professional colleague, Larry Rottmann, on *Voices From The Ho Chi Minh Trail*. It is my desire—as well as the desire of the Vietnamese people—that these poems and photographs will help lead to more healing between our two peoples. This book clearly reveals, for both sides, the cost of war, and price of peace. But at the same time, it is a work of humanity, suffused with love for the future, where all of our children will live.

Nguyen Trong Thanh
Hanoi, Vietnam
1993

THE POEMS

THE PHOTOGRAPHS